This Much Very

Hiram Larew

ISBN: 9798339683018

Hiram Larew 2024

©™®

Alien Buddha Press 2024

abuddahpress@yahoo.com

Dedicated to every dint of.

Contents

Wilt or Stray	9
Drenched	10
Growing Up	11
Believe Cedars	13
Needed to Fly	15
Hollywood	16
Smokey Arms	18
In Ames, Iowa	20
Angelic	21
Grit River	23
Gold Begins	24
Wrong Things	26
One More Time	27
Right Here Right Now	28
Wheat Dust	30
As Float As	31
Tangled	32
New York City	33
Jewelweed	34
Dint Of	35
Maybe Jilted	36
Front Porch Lights	38
They Already Have	39
To the Limit	41
Senses More Of	42
Acknowledgments and Bio	44

***

This Much Very by Hiram Larew invites you to stretch beyond the expected. This is poetry where the familiar is wrapped in something strange and the strange becomes a doorway into something unpredictable.

Larew's verses whisper, sing, and sometimes shout, all while pulling you deeper into the rhythm of their peculiar charm. The themes here—connection, time, longing—are explored with a light poetic touch.

The language in this chapbook bends and curls in ways that feel at once new and timeless, with just a twist of phrase. Whether you're a lover of lyrical puzzles, a seeker of quiet epiphanies, or someone who enjoys words for the pure joy of how they sound together, **This Much Very** will speak to you.

***

Wilt or Stray

I am incredibly lucky --
   even this haze knows it
   even my useless gaze says so
   in every way.

To be where I am now
   living like this
   is like cherries on a branch.

In fact I'm not nearly grateful enough
   for this mud and for its reasons.

Not thankful enough for fences down
   or kinked hoses.

No I don't deserve porches.

In fact I need to tip my hat in love and honor
   to every buzzing swarm that's coming at me
   to every wilt or stray.

And I should also surely thank my lucky stars
   my blessings
   for what last night had its way
   with the row of beans out back
   in the garden.

Drenched

You are god-soaked --
    a hay dream that
    drenches the prairies and that
    all haloes pour through

You are hope atmospheric and
    raw storms inviting
    that overwhelm echoes and what's mighty

Or vast hallows and
    flood fields that
    rush holy forward
    with you

Yes you are a torch-trumpeted cloud --
    the choicest swoon specter
    that sounds out alive
    through what's purest of downpours

And whenever you run for cover
    under thundering goodness
    all rakes get tossed love-like
    up in the air

Growing Up

        I'm not tellin' you again Natalie Ray Jones
        To get your fat butt over here now girl
        Get the hell out of those weeds and come here

But Mama I love them. James says they're ferns like learns.
And Mama

        I don't give a fat fit about nothing ferns or learns
        girl. Get over here now before I come in there
        and sack you flat out. You don't want me to
        come over there. I'm tellin' you you do not
        want me to come in there to get you. This is the
        last time I swear to god I'm tellin' you girl. I'm
        not your mother for nothin'. Hear me?

Ok Mama but can I bring some?

        What! Bring some of those weeds? Where girl?
        I know you're not *that* crazy. Maybe simple.
        But not crazy enough to carry weeds
        and bug spit into *my* house. Oh no.

But Mama I love them. Look. They're even over there where
there's water. All over. I've never seen them before and

        Don't talk back to me, missy thing. I don't care
        squat about you seein' that crap. Now I am
        tellin' you for the very last time to stop prancing
        around and get your big butt back over here

now. How did you get off this road anyway without me seein'?

Wait a minute. Someone's callin'– oh it's Leon. Say what? I can't hear you. Wait a minute. Yeah I know. Crap. It's some kinda truck comin' and I can't hear you. And Sweet Little Miss Nothing Natalie is over in the damn woods and won't get her lazy ass out. What? Well don't tell me what to do. I heard you the first time. Leon why don't you drag your smelly little ass to work. Just piss the hell off Leon.

Natalie get over here girl or I'm skinning you alive for dinner. Now. Yes right now I said.

Believe Cedars

I come soft barely to Burden Lake its
Birch shore and hear
Children across the water splashing for fun as
A motor boat throttles back when it
Rounds buoys

I sit under a branch halfway that is asking to
Have its picture taken with
The water

Why not I say as the piper cub cuts
The sky's corner and
The breeze takes the
Leaves on a lark like my mind

In fact if I was younger I'd try
To swim to
The island out there maybe
A fourth of a mile away floating
I believe on cedars

The fact that I'm not fully
Here and won't visit again makes
The lake seem even larger

I see that someone has cut the grass around
Me and that brambles and
Today's cares are just beyond me and
Yes here comes a pair of ducks uninvited
Thank goodness

How do I prepare on
Burden Lake's edge for
The long run or for glistening especially
When I hold my breath in my arms while
The outboard motor waves from its deck

Hello

Needed to Fly

You pointed out
So often
That no matter what else happens
Roots will keep digging deeper.

And many many times when things had gone to zero
You'd say *Just try to listen*
And you'd wink.

In fact, once when going up some steps that were dicey
You turned around and nodded at me --
Whatever was coming or about to happen
Solid or not
Seemed like air turning bright blue
To you.

So just about now
You must be trying to send at least
A speck of common sense my way
I hope
Or anything else
That helped you to fly beyond.

And yes
Knowing you and where you are now
I'm convinced that everything that's still here
And deserving
Like grief or snow or magic
Will finally get some well-earned rest.

Hollywood

For sure
I'd pull out my last tooth to be that tall dark and handsome
And yes even be willing to die real young
    just so I could live on and on
    in movie posters

But before that
I'd like to have the kind of looks
    that would stop nearly anything breathing in its tracks
    as it stared at me and my marvel --
        at my boat-load of handy dandy
        and my big cup running over
        if you get my drift

I swear
I'd give my good eye to be an eyeful
    of a best-looking swoon angel
The kind of *oh my goodness* that's like
    when butter meets honey
    for sure

Yes my magazine looks
    would and should be the best ever seen
    since hair was parted by Moses
    or someone Egyptian

I'd even give a twist on this bad thumb to be *irresistible*
And yes, that's spelled like a parade float
    with a real sexy *i* waving up front
    and a big bad *e* grinning in the rear

    if you get my drift

Truly I'd give up my last smoke
    the very best one I'm told
To have god idol looks
So that whenever however and as ever I went
    every living soul
      would pay to climb up trees
      for the precious gold chance to see me

Smokey Arms

Lately I've been amazed by my father's memory
As I remember him --

He could recall as brightly as the skins of apples
How his father was certain but quiet
My father also knew by heart what the snow looked like
On those very steps
Where he first spied my mother
And he had an uncanny way as well
Of remembering where the smallest creeks cross
In West Virginia

More and more it's as if my father is sitting
On the edge of a bed in boxers
Or is stoking a nearby fire telling stories

More and more I think of him as very sure
Like me
Of people even before he ever met them
And of course he was squirrely eyed about
Anyone in power

In fact as I think back
It's almost as if my father has been
Lifted up in the chilly air by some smokey arms
As a favor

That's all to say that there's nothing
He wouldn't have done
For bright foggy mornings like this --

Ones that start heading out
But then have to turn back around on a damn dime
To go all the way home
Chuckling
For whatever it was
That was forgotten.

In Ames, Iowa

If I was to give you something simple
What would it be
What could I bring you --

I might pull up onions
From a spot I know
For bundles
Because they aren't given away
As they should be
And they might surprise you

Or I might
Better get you something easy
Say a good map or a flashlight
That could come in handy
At some point

But then again
Those all seem too much like you

So maybe something with magic in it
Like the barn's hay

The trick is to find a gift that
Won't overdo you

I know --
How about if somehow I bring you
That mix I just saw
Of sunshine on mud

Angelic

I am of you very --
    harked and wildly
    yes and hovered
    raised on twirls and wonder
My arms above are lifted with you
    to over flowing

Here my heart is fully spread
    or split or stirred beyond you
    even beyond unending pieces

And I am wings as much as any --
    all above you
    higher than what may almost be

I blaze all towards your eyes of light
    and flings
    as moths of love come closer
On this fizzling air
    forever forward rising on and on --
    I fly unto you

Yes I am of you ever
    in swept up breath
    in shudders timeless
    as you daze the purely --
So radiantly and scattered by
    or lifted high through such craze

For I am come to you on trumpets

and by or for you always
as if for wings to see or tell
of singing skies that climb
in countless heavens of you

Grit Rivers

How poems are nets
That let crows fly through
But not sparrows
And fishes like time
Come to reckon
With catching some
But others let go

    And how poems make meshes
    Of tangles

What is it that happens
With *not now* or *come see*
And every *has to be* --
Yes poems catch to lose
Don't they

    Yes the sifting things
    Are poems that matter
    Like flour to yeast -- its power
    Or like what branches do
    Weaving the sun

Poems even kneel
By grit rivers
Some long ago with pans
For nuggets of mountains
Making secret discoveries --
Their gleeful dripping hands
Shaking to share the news

Gold Begins

Yes your highness
Your history will be told
By wondrous sunrise

Indeed believe me your grace --
What will endear you to the ages
Is a magnificence that every gem in your crown
Will proclaim again and again
And your time will be deeply recalled
As the kind of gold that is forever exalted

So I entreat you to trust me --
You will go on towards a bright dawn
Revered one
In a thousand ways

Oh and yes as your reign flies forth into time's mist
Just imagine the glistening throne awaiting
And how all will obey and shine true before it
As accounts are told and then retold of your remarkable era --
Its prosper and conquests

Yes even as you nibble that toast my liege
Just imagine such heavenly bounty

And take comfort –
Even your long ago childhood
Will return gilded as sunbeams
Again and again I am certain
Yes up there your eminence
Up there in sweetness
Your years will surely command the skies

And your wisdom and words will be enshrined
Beyond any future or earthly measures

So rest gently your majesty --
I am here to assure you that
Should you stay in bed now or even always
In lasting comforts
There is a beyond and hereafter waiting for you

And in fact I know this surely --
That all manner of legends
Will enter your chamber this evening like servants
Their hands outstretched
Begging your grace with sweet pleas and silver
To let them – these legends –
Be a speck in the glory
Of what you will become

Wrong Things

I need to listen more to wrong things. Yes
I need to let talk that's hard get
        close to me.
I need to believe in the truth of burned up dinners and
        take lessons from dogs that
        sneak by with ticks.

In fact the only way I'll learn
        probably is from
        an animal that's hurt or from
        a kid who's shaky scared
Yes the hollow sounds they make turn
        my shivers into wisdom.

So with all of that in mind I think
        I'll turn my back on the
        surest things in life because
It seems
        along comes a mistake or
        bams of angry lightning and
What had been neat and locked down tight
        splits apart
        wide open all at once
        with over-flowing concerns yes
        but also with revelations.

One More Time

Here we go again…

I never said anything
Not even nothing
        about thin or fat
        or sloppy or neat
        or give or take

Nothing

All I said is that
When I opened the door
What I saw last night of you
        looked like radio static
        wrapped in wet newspapers
        at the bottom of a long hard swig

So ok go ahead and get to it
Tell me one more time
Why my grandmother
        who left this earth eagerly
        many decades ago
        is to blame
        for everything

Right Here Right Now

As he was climbing the garden wall
Romeo in all legends
And moonlight
Began to realize deep down and surely
The glorious power of his arms
And so he flew up beyond himself
In love
Oh yes he did
Even though he was and still is
Just smoke

And when too
Almost as long ago
One of the most fabled explorers alive
Finally found freshets of water
In the desert
Gurgling like sighs
There must have been a cry in his heart
Yes a love in flight
That can never ever be described in tales gone by
No matter what

So then when
Beyond all discovery
The only daybreak in the world blooms
And flows
Right here right now
On your shoulder
To rise in my arms
In a story

Is it any surprise
That even the clouds shake their heads
And say oh no oh no
There are too many wings already

Wheat Dust

Only thing I can think of as bad off as me
Is harvest.
Yes it's as flat as my face
And just about as friendly as a dead rock.
Try making anything out of this wheat dust
If you will.

Someone said just yesterday that my eyes look bad.
Well of course they do from no water.

Crows could tell you as much.
They're not dumb.
No rain and they're gone.
They've got good sense.
Fact is they flew off months ago
When the going was good,
When I was still sleeping on the box springs
For the love of pete
But not anymore.

Let me say again about what a joy it is
To be sleeping flat on the floor.
Right down there with the mice and their musties.

I tell you if I didn't have Jimmy
I'd leave too.

Damn I would.

Something will happen.

As Float As

One reason this note is
    whatever floats by
    as can be
Is man alive inside me
    with as much try as I can

Yes I'd give this heart to see
    a *by chance* waving
    or to hear *believe me* sounds in trees

All so that from clear to bright
    these *what dreams are madeof* ways
    could shake me awake

In fact whenever *must do*
    calls me
Or *yes right now* swoops in to ride alongside me
Then indeed I become
    again and again

It's as if when I feel forever
    diving deep down inside me
    as it should
That my yes and again
    go up larking
    all loop-de-loop
    like this note
    more to fully

Tangled

There are just too many worlds out there –
Ones as bald as buzzards
And others tangled up in vines
Most as cold as a pirate's grin
Or as orange as blue can be
Some mornings

Yes there are too many worlds calling –
With every *See you later* sounding
A little like a charm
Or with their love pitched up in the wind
Like straw

And there are too many worlds warning –
With wasps swarming overhead
Or scissors pointing
And with sirens lighting the way
At night

Sometimes overall
With this much very
There are just too many worlds trying --
With trees begging the sky for love
Or peaches desperate for cream
Or even more than that
With that gushing
That just won't stop gushing *Why*.

New York City

    I've often wondered
    What it would be like
    To be the kind of smart that's dumb
    To talk math on rush hour corners
    Or to be a child laughing to herself
    On museum steps
    To even be steam shooting sideways
    From somewhere above --
    Yes so smart that you nearly hiss

        In fact as I get older I don't learn as much
        From big bridges over rivers
        Or understand
        What billboards overhead want of me

But I do feel better
Knowing that somehow
Someone just ahead has figured out a way
To stack up
Too many pipes on his shoulder.

Jewelweed

The first time I saw someone like me
    was on a farm --
There was a shagbark hickory overhead
And wrapped up sandwiches somewhere
I believe

I was just starting to look at
    anything whistling

And as I recall he was wearing two strings --
    one in a knot around his wrist
    and the other tied to my dreams.

Fast forward to this moment in a city's bustle
    with stacked up skies and sidewalks that cram

The more I try to figure out
    who's me in this crowd --
    buzzes and whistles --
    the more my eyes go beyond me.

And also there's the difference between
    these outspoken grins I see today
    and those guesses of lips from long ago
    that opened me up like jewelweed --

The difference seems wondrously between
    what might have been
    and oh no never

Dint Of

What comes of waiting for
      or holding on

Or of if and when
      or chances paused and wished for

What comes true from shy aways
      and try and try or overdues

What comes about while counting down
      or passing through

And what comes from
      coulds or mights

Yes what happens even after every dint of

And then with all of those
And at first
What comes with daylights of find --
      like shoes of love
          that socks search and search for

Maybe Jilted

Don't I already have enough green in me?
Enough trees in clouds?
Enough tendrils that call me?

Is there an end to how much mud I can love?
Or dew I can keep?
Or trails that will hike me
Up over the hill?

Sometimes it seems I've done this enough
Even too often --
I've argued with moss and heard duff sigh
And I've pinched ticks in forests
In fact I've even vowed to myself on ledges
Many times over
And yes I've always loved it all.

But for some reason this time
As I look downstream
It begins to sink in
That creeks don't believe me
And these ferns don't know me
They don't have to
And what's rustling up in the branches
Is too far beyond.

Suddenly I realize that the trees' memo to me
Is simple
It says --
We'll get back to you

Maybe
If we ever want to --
In a bedrock sort of way.

And so all at once I feel pretty honest
Even a little crucial
And maybe just slightly jilted
By this mile-long foot path
That's wandering with me

So then for the first time ever
I decide to sass them back --
I thank the lichens politely
For their service
But in the same breath
Remind them that
I really don't need them
Because there's a hot cup of coffee waiting for me
Back home.

Front Porch Lights

Lord god am I ever so glad to have bad weather
To talk about
And also all of those moths that keep swarming
At night
That I can bring up and mention

Because otherwise who knows
How much more fuss and tussle
About flag-waving fluff
There would be to put up with
At church
Or the hair parlor
Or in too-long checkout lines

Yes thank gracious for any high winds predicted
(Or better yet hail)
Or those bright porch lightbulbs
And all that they do moth-wise
To help me keep the riled up chatter diverged
And off topic
At least for now

Amen

They Already Have

I'm not sure where these new can't do's
Came from
But just like how autumn sends signals
My veins have started to stoop
And lately my grins are having second thoughts

And yes if it calls at all
Loves calls from dusty roads

There's less of what's always been always
And everything's beginning to slant

Said otherwise
My trees are acting more like roots

And I'm not sure deep down
Of what will change next
And become limits

In fact what I'm finding
Is that a tiny twinge today
Can turn into huge trouble tomorrow
In fact it already has

So because I can't predict
When I will no longer be able
To reach up high or do things
I'll tell you a good story now
While I can
About someone who jumps into the river

Of course feet first
Yes
Holding their breath
But all the while
Shouting out loud

To the Limit

Someone asks what I would fight for ...

Well I'd fight for the moon in a heartbeat
With its halo of wisdom
Its cloud-cover of guess
And its wish to
Even its merely
Yes I'd march for its glowing

And I'd defend the moon with longings
With anything I could muster
No limits --
To keep it up over
For harvests or phases
Even for no one

Then if allowed to
I'd rejoice in its quiet apart from
That always wins me --
The moon's mix of far away but right there
All gathered around --
For as long as what matters
Lets me

Senses More Of

What I would give for a poem's line
To love me --
To wake me unknowing with
What time it is
And hum words of purple for me
Or write what's new by rise

        What I would do for that kind
        Of love that shies for sounds
        Or rhymes more of me than I have

I would vow so my heart
So my days and any phrases
To say that much
If I could

        Yes for that gift of once
        I would pledge my dreams and bounds
        For the chance to wake
        Beside a poem's shoulder.

Poems in this collection first appeared in the following journals or anthologies.

* Poetry Bus * Juste Literary Magazine * Poetry Catalog *
* Backchannels * San Antonio Review * Flat Ink Magazine *
* The Gilded Weathervane * Empyrean Literary Magazine *
* River Road Poetry Anthology * The Winged Moon *
* Prairie Home Magazine * Fowl Feathered Review *
* The Universes Poetry Literary Journal * Pride Poem Podcast *
* WriteNow Literary Journal *

Hiram Larew's poetry appears widely. His most recent collection, *Patchy Ways*, was published by CyberWit Press in 2023. As founder of Poetry X Hunger, he's bringing a world of poets to the anti-hunger cause.

www.HiramLarewPoetry.com and www.PoetryXHunger.com

Made in the USA
Middletown, DE
26 January 2025